The French Cat

A Fireside Book
Published by SIMON AND SCHUSTER • NEW YORK

A Fireside Book
Published by Simon and Schuster
A Division of Gulf & Western Corporation
Simon & Schuster Building
Rockefeller Center
1230 Avenue of the Americas
New York, New York 10020
FIRESIDE and colophon are trademarks
of Simon and Schuster

Manufactured in the United States of America

1 3 5 7 9 10 8 6 4 2 Pbk.

Library of Congress Cataloging in Publication Data

Siné.
The French cat.

"A Fireside book."
1. Cats—Caricatures and cartoons.   2. French
wit and humor, Pictorial.   I. Title.
NC1499.S5A4   1982   741.5'944   82-6013
                                                AACR2

ISBN 0-671-45693-8

THIS is a French Cat—

entre-chat

There will be more French Cats, and
some International Cats—but, first, here are...

41 American Cats

cat nip

cat apult

Catalina

cat astrophy

fraidy cat

cat gut

cat bird

cat fish

holy cats

Cat ullus (84-54 B.C.)

s'cat

Al cat raz

cat sup

vindi cat ive

provo cat ive

deli cat essen

cat arrh

cat arrh (2)

puss café

cat alog

cat o nine tails

cat a lyst

s cat ology

cat's cradle

wild cat

wildcat

cat e gory

platy puss

fat cat

cat alan

cat skills

Œdi puss

Œdi puss complex

catty corner

Kitty Hawk

Cat herine the Great

Bruce Cat ton

cat erpillar

cat er pillar (2)

cat in jthe[?]

cat erpillar (3)

cat ching

Popo cat epetl

French Cats

chat teau

chat peau

chat steté

chat teaubriand

chat timent

Mon premier est un
Chat
Mon deuxième est un
Chat
Mon troisième est un
Chat
et mon tout est une
Danse:

chat rade

chat cha cha

pa chat

chat monix

chat riot

chat grin

chat seur

chat sœur

chat blis

Chat peron rouge

Chat rlemagne

Chat plin

Chat kespeare

Chat liapine

Chat gall

Chat s'Addams

International Cats

rick chat

gei chat

Ra chat mon

Chat tanooga choo choo

cat - cciatore

Louis Cat orze

G.B. Chat

Cat chat turian

Chat-tauqua

chat - lelegh

chat-d roe

Ror chat k